easy meals

potatoes

BARNES
&NOBLE
BOOKS
NEW YORK

This edition published by Barnes & Noble Inc.,
by arrangement with Parragon

2002 Barnes & Noble Books

M 1 0 9 8 7 6 5 4 3 2 1

ISBN: 0-7607-3298-1

Printed in Spain

Produced by The Bridgewater Book Company Ltd, Lewes, East Sussex, United Kingdom

Acknowledgements
Creative Director Terry Jeavons
Art Director Sarah Howerd
Editorial Director Fiona Biggs
Senior Editor Mark Truman
Editorial Assistants Simon Bailey, Tom Kitch
Page Make-up Chris Akroyd

NOTES FOR THE READER

- This book uses both US and metric measurements. Follow the same units of measurement throughout; do not mix US and metric.
- All spoon measurements are level: teaspoons are assumed to be 5 ml, and table-spoons are assumed to be 15 ml.
- Cup measurements in this book are for American cups.
- Unless otherwise stated, milk is assumed to be whole milk, eggs and individual vegetables such as potatoes are medium-sized, and pepper is freshly ground black pepper.
- Recipes using raw or very lightly cooked eggs should be avoided by infants, the elderly, pregnant women, convalescents, and anyone suffering from an illness.
- Optional ingredients, variations or serving suggestions have not been included in the calculations.
- The times given are an approximate guide only. Preparation times differ according to the techniques used by different people, and the cooking times vary as a result of the type of oven used.

Contents

Introduction

Potatoes are perhaps the most versatile of all vegetables. Not only can they be served in a wide variety of ways to accompany a main course but they can also be an integral part of a main course. A vegetable, meat, or fish base, topped with mashed potatoes and cheese, and baked in the oven until crisp and golden, makes a wonderful homely and comforting dish. Potatoes add just the right amount of body to a smooth soup, and contribute a satisfying chunkiness to a thick, hearty soup. New potatoes are delicious boiled and then cooled to use in a salad. They can even be transformed into a base to be used as an alternative to a dough base for a pizza. Potato & Pepperoni Pizza is ideal for pizza lovers who have a gluten intolerance.

There are many varieties of potato, so always select a suitable potato for a dish you plan to cook. Be guided by the ingredients

guide to recipe key	
easy	Recipes are graded as follows: 1 pea—easy; 2 peas—very easy; 3 peas—extremely easy.
serves 4	Most of the recipes in this book serve four people. Simply halve the ingredients to serve two, taking care not to mix US and metric measurements.
15 minutes	Preparation time. Where recipes include soaking, standing, or poaching, times for these are listed separately: eg, 15 minutes, plus 30 minutes to stand.
15 minutes	Cooking time. Cooking times do not include the cooking of rice, noodles, or vegetables served with the main dishes.

list that accompanies each recipe. Waxy potatoes hold their shape during cooking—when sliced and cooked on top of a hotpot or a pie, or when panfried for a Spanish tortilla. Mealy potatoes soften while cooking, so they are ideal for mashing to use as a topping and for binding fish cakes and nut roasts. They also absorb other flavors readily, so they are perfect for spicy dishes, such as Spicy Potato & Rice Pilaf, or Indian Potato Salad. Sweet potatoes may be served with savory dishes, or teamed with bananas to make a deliciously different warm Sweet Potato & Banana Salad, with a honey, lemon, and chive dressing.

Potato, Sausage & Onion Pie, page 44

Soups

Potatoes appear in many classic soup recipes. An old favorite is leek & potato soup, or Vichyssoise, which may be served hot or chilled, but an interesting variation of this is Celery Root, Leek & Potato Soup. Celery root is a knobbly root vegetable, which may look unpromising, but has a subtle celery flavor. Another classic to be found in the following pages is Cullen Skink from Scotland ("skink" means "soup"), a thick, creamy, fish soup made from cod and smoked haddock. It is warming and satisfying, but also luxurious.

Celery Root, Leek & Potato Soup

INGREDIENTS

1 tbsp butter
1 onion, chopped
2 large leeks, halved
    lengthwise and sliced
1 large celery root
    (about 1 lb 10 oz/
    750 g), peeled
    and cubed
1 potato, cubed
1 carrot, cut into four
    and sliced thinly
5 cups water
1/8 tsp dried marjoram
1 bay leaf
freshly grated nutmeg
salt and pepper
celery leaves, to garnish

❶ Melt the butter in a large pan over a medium–low heat. Add the onion and leeks, and panfry for about 4 minutes, stirring frequently, until they just soften. Do not let the onion and leek color.

❷ Add the celery root, potato, carrot, water, marjoram, and bay leaf, and a large pinch of salt. Bring to a boil, reduce the heat, cover the pan, and simmer for about 25 minutes until the vegetables are tender. Remove the bay leaf.

❸ Allow the soup to cool slightly. Transfer to a blender or a food processor, and purée until smooth. (If using a food processor, strain off the cooking liquid and reserve. Purée the soup solids with enough cooking liquid to moisten them, then combine with remaining liquid.)

❹ Return the puréed soup to the pan, and stir to blend. Season with salt, pepper, and nutmeg. Simmer over a medium–low heat until the soup is reheated.

❺ Ladle the soup into warm bowls, and garnish with celery leaves. Serve immediately, piping hot.

 very easy

serves 4

15 minutes

 45 minutes

Roasted Garlic & Potato Soup

INGREDIENTS

1 large bulb of garlic
    with large cloves,
    peeled (about
    3½ oz/100 g)
2 tsp olive oil
2 large leeks,
    sliced thinly
1 large onion,
    chopped finely
3 potatoes, diced
    (about 1 lb 2 oz/
    500 g)
5 cups chicken or
    vegetable bouillon
1 bay leaf
⅔ cup light cream
freshly grated nutmeg
fresh lemon juice
    (optional)
salt and pepper
snipped fresh chives,
    to garnish

❶ Put the garlic cloves on a cookie sheet, brush lightly with oil, and bake in a preheated oven at 350°F/180°C for about 20 minutes until they turn golden.

❷ Heat the oil in a large pan over a medium heat. Add the leeks and onion, cover the pan, and cook for about 3 minutes, stirring frequently, until they begin to soften.

❸ Add the potatoes, roasted garlic, bouillon, and bay leaf. Season as necessary with salt and pepper. Bring to a boil, reduce the heat, cover the pan, and simmer the soup gently for about 30 minutes until the vegetables are tender. Remove the bay leaf.

❹ Allow the soup to cool slightly, then transfer it to a blender or a food processor and blend until smooth, working in batches if necessary. (If using a food processor, strain off the cooking liquid and reserve. Purée the soup solids with enough cooking liquid to moisten them, then combine with the remaining liquid.)

❺ Return the soup to the pan and stir in the cream and a generous grating of nutmeg. Taste, and adjust the seasoning, if necessary, adding a few drops of lemon juice, if wished. Warm the soup over a low heat. Ladle into warm soup bowls, garnish with chives or parsley, and serve.

 very easy

 serves 4

10 minutes

 1 hour

Sweet Potato, Apple & Leek Soup

INGREDIENTS

1 tbsp butter
3 leeks, sliced thinly
1 large carrot, sliced
   thinly
2 sweet potatoes,
   peeled and cubed
2 large tart apples
   (about 1 lb 5 oz/
   600 g), peeled
   and cubed
5 cups water
freshly grated nutmeg
1 cup apple juice
1 cup whipping or
   light cream
salt and pepper
snipped fresh chives
   or cilantro,
   to garnish

❶ Melt the butter in a large pan over a medium–low heat. Add the leeks, cover the pan, and cook for 6–8 minutes, or until the leek softens, stirring frequently.

❷ Add the carrot, sweet potatoes, apples, and water. Add salt, pepper, and nutmeg to taste. Bring to a boil, reduce the heat, and simmer, covered, for about 20 minutes, or until the vegetables are very tender, stirring occasionally.

❸ Let the soup cool slightly, then transfer to a blender or a food processor, and purée until smooth, working in batches if necessary. (If using a food processor, strain off the cooking liquid and reserve. Purée the soup solids with enough cooking liquid to moisten them, then combine with the remaining liquid.)

❹ Return the puréed soup to the pan and stir in the apple juice. Place on a low heat and simmer for about 10 minutes until heated through.

❺ Stir in the cream and continue simmering for about 5 minutes, stirring frequently, until heated through. Taste and adjust the seasoning, adding more salt, pepper, and nutmeg, if necessary. Ladle the soup into warm bowls, garnish with chives or cilantro, and serve.

 very easy

 serves 4

 10 minutes

45 minutes

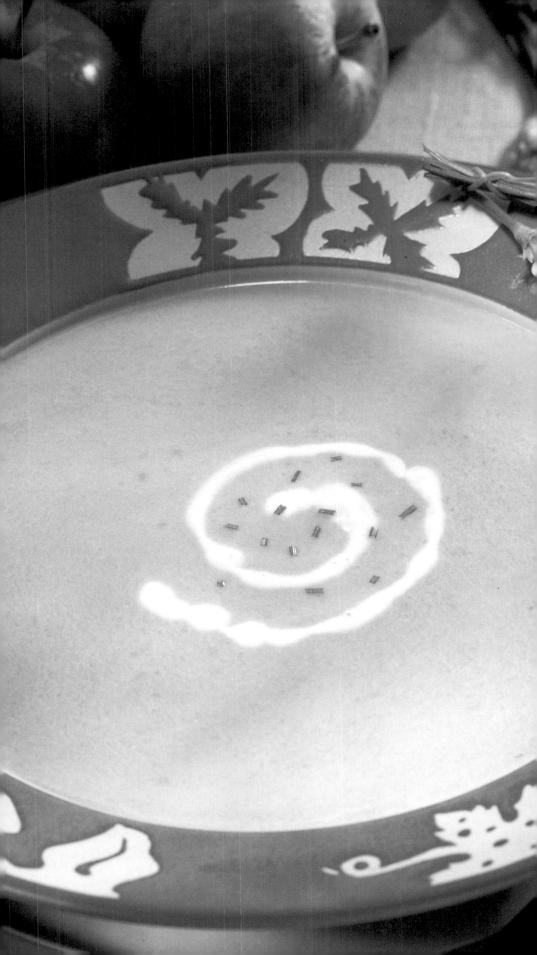

Smoked Haddock & Potato Soup

1 tbsp oil
2 oz/55 g bacon, cut
*   into thin strips*
1 large onion,
*   chopped finely*
2 tbsp all-purpose flour
4 cups milk
1 lb 9 oz/700 g
*   potatoes, cut into*
*   ½ inch/1.2 cm cubes*
6 oz/175 g skinless
*   smoked haddock*
salt and pepper
finely chopped fresh
*   parsley, to garnish*

 very easy

 serves 4

 5–10 minutes

 40 minutes

❶ Heat the oil in a large pan over a medium heat. Add the bacon, and panfry for 2 minutes. Stir in the onion and continue cooking for 5–7 minutes, stirring frequently, until the onion is soft and the bacon golden. Tip the pan and spoon off as much fat as possible.

❷ Stir in the flour and continue cooking for 2 minutes. Add half of the milk and stir well, scraping the bottom of the pan to mix in the flour.

❸ Add the potatoes and the remaining milk, and season with pepper. Bring just to a boil, stirring frequently. Reduce the heat and simmer, partially covered, for 10 minutes.

❹ Add the fish and continue simmering, stirring occasionally, for about 15 minutes, or until the potatoes are tender and the fish breaks up easily.

❺ Taste the soup and adjust the seasoning (salt may not be needed). Ladle into a warm tureen or bowls, and sprinkle generously with chopped parsley.

COOK'S TIP
Cutting the potatoes into small cubes not only looks attractive, but it also lets them cook more quickly and evenly.

Spicy Potato & Garbanzo Soup

INGREDIENTS

1 tbsp olive oil
1 large onion,
    chopped finely
2–3 garlic cloves,
    chopped finely or
    crushed
1 carrot, cut into four
    and sliced thinly
12 oz/350 g potatoes,
    diced
¼ tsp ground turmeric
¼ tsp garam masala
¼ tsp mild curry powder
14 oz/400 g canned
    chopped tomatoes
3¾ cups water
¼ tsp chili paste
14 oz/400 g canned
    garbanzos, rinsed
    and drained
3 oz/85 g fresh peas,
    or frozen peas,
    defrosted
salt and pepper
chopped fresh cilantro,
    to garnish

❶ Heat the olive oil in a large pan over a medium heat. Add the onion and garlic, and cook for 3–4 minutes, stirring occasionally, until the onion begins to soften.

❷ Add the carrot, potatoes, turmeric, garam masala, and curry powder, and continue cooking for 1–2 minutes.

❸ Add the tomatoes, water, chili paste, and a large pinch of salt. Reduce the heat, cover the pan, and simmer for 30 minutes, stirring occasionally.

❹ Add the garbanzos and peas to the pan, continue cooking for about 15 minutes, or until all the vegetables are tender.

❺ Taste the soup and adjust the seasoning, if necessary, adding a little more chili to taste. Ladle into warm soup bowls and sprinkle with cilantro.

 very easy

 serves 4

 5 minutes

 50 minutes

Green Lentil, Potato & Ham Soup

INGREDIENTS

10½ oz/300 g Puy lentils
2 tsp butter
1 large onion, chopped
     finely
2 carrots, chopped finely
1 garlic clove, chopped
2 cups water
1 bay leaf
¼ tsp dried sage or
     rosemary
4 cups chicken bouillon
8 oz/225 g potatoes,
     diced (see Cook's Tip)
1 tbsp tomato paste
4 oz/115 g smoked ham,
     diced finely
salt and pepper
chopped fresh parsley,
     to garnish

 very easy

 serves 5

 10–15minutes

 45 minutes

COOK'S TIP
Cut the potatoes into small cubes, about ¾ inch/5 mm, so they will be in proportion to the lentils.

❶ Rinse and drain the lentils, then check for small stones, and remove them.

❷ Melt the butter in a large pan or flameproof casserole over a medium heat. Add the onion, carrots, and garlic, cover the pan, and panfry, stirring frequently, for 4–5 minutes until the onion softens slightly.

❸ Add the lentils to the vegetables with the water, bay leaf, and sage or rosemary. Bring to a boil, reduce the heat, cover and simmer for 10 minutes.

❹ Add the bouillon, potatoes, tomato paste, and ham. Bring back to a simmer. Cover the pan and simmer for another 25–30 minutes, or until the vegetables are tender.

❺ Season with salt and pepper and remove the bay leaf. Ladle into warm bowls, garnish with parsley, and serve.

Cullen Skink

INGREDIENTS

*8 oz/225 g smoked
  haddock fillet
2 tbsp butter
1 onion, chopped finely
2½ cups milk
12 oz/350 g potatoes,
  diced
12 oz/350 g cod, boned,
  skinned, and cubed
⅔ cup heavy cream
2 tbsp chopped fresh
  parsley
lemon juice, to taste
salt and pepper*

GARNISH
*lemon slices
parsley sprigs*

very easy

serves 4

20 minutes

35 minutes,
plus 10 minutes
to poach

COOK'S TIP
Rather than use
yellow-dyed haddock
fillet, which may be
whiting and not
haddock at all, look
for Finnan haddock.

❶ Put the haddock fillet in a large skillet and cover with boiling water. Let stand for 10 minutes. Drain, reserving 1 cup of the soaking water. Flake the fish, taking care to remove all the bones.

❷ Heat the butter in a large pan and add the onion. Cook gently for 10 minutes until soft. Add the milk and bring to a gentle simmer, then add the potato and cook it gently for 10 minutes.

❸ Add the reserved haddock flakes and the cod. Simmer another 10 minutes until the cod is tender.

❹ Remove about one third of the fish and potatoes, put in a food processor, and blend until smooth. Alternatively, push through a sieve into a bowl. Return to the soup with the cream and parsley. Season and add a little lemon juice to taste. Add a little of the reserved soaking water if the soup seems too thick. Reheat gently and serve at once, garnished with lemon slices and parsley sprigs.

New England Clam Chowder

INGREDIENTS

2 lb/900 g live clams
4 slices bacon, chopped
2 tbsp butter
1 onion, chopped
1 tbsp chopped fresh
  thyme
1 large potato, diced
1¼ cups milk
1 bay leaf
1⅔ cups heavy cream
1 tbsp chopped fresh
  parsley
salt and pepper
reserve 8 clams in their
  shells, to garnish
  (see Cook's Tip)

easy

serves 4

15 minutes

30 minutes

❶ Scrub the clams and put them into a large pan with a splash of water. Cook over a high heat for 3–4 minutes until they open. Discard any that remain closed. Strain, reserving the cooking liquid. Set aside until cool enough to handle.

❷ Remove the clams from their shells, chopping them roughly if they are large, and set aside.

❸ In a clean pan, fry the bacon until browned and crisp. Drain on paper towels. Add the butter to the same pan, and when it has melted, add the onion. Panfry for 4–5 minutes until soft but not colored. Add the thyme and cook briefly before adding the diced potato, reserved clam cooking liquid, milk, and bay leaf. Bring to a boil and simmer for 10 minutes until the potato is just tender.

❹ Transfer to a food processor and blend until smooth, or push through a sieve into a bowl.

❺ Add the reserved clams, the bacon, and the cream. Simmer for another 2–3 minutes until heated through. Season to taste. Stir in the chopped parsley, and serve, garnished with clams in their shells.

COOK'S TIP
A smart way of presenting this dish is to sit 2 of the reserved clams in their shells on top of each bowl of soup before serving.

Main Meals

If meals based on potatoes evoke images of snacks and midweek meals, the recipes in this section will give you plenty of ideas for converting them into elegant appetizers and main-course dishes for weekend lunches and dinners. Veal Italienne is a casserole cooked with red wine, tomatoes, olives, and basil, the perennially popular ingredients of Italian cuisine. For a special potato dish to serve vegetarian guests, try Potato-Topped Vegetables in Wine. The distinctive flavor of fennel in the base is echoed by fennel seeds in the cheese and potato topping.

Quick Chicken Bake

INGREDIENTS

1 lb 2 oz/500 g ground
   chicken
1 large onion, chopped
   finely
2 carrots, diced finely
2 tbsp all-purpose flour
1 tbsp tomato paste
1¼ cups chicken
   bouillon
pinch of fresh thyme
2 lb/900 g potatoes,
   cooked, and mashed
   with butter and milk,
   and well seasoned
¾ cup grated Cheddar
   cheese
salt and pepper
peas, to serve

1 Dry-fry the ground chicken, onion, and carrots in a non-stick skillet for 5 minutes to brown them, stirring frequently.

2 Sprinkle the chicken with the flour, and simmer for another 2 minutes.

3 Blend in the tomato paste and bouillon a little at a time, then simmer for 15 minutes. Season, then add the thyme.

4 Transfer the chicken and vegetable mixture to an ovenproof casserole and let cool.

5 Spoon the mashed potato over the chicken mixture and sprinkle with the cheese. Bake in a preheated oven, 400°F/200°C for 20 minutes, or until the cheese is bubbling and golden, then serve with the peas.

 very easy

 serves 4

 10 minutes,
plus 15 minutes
to cool

 45 minutes

COOK'S TIP
As an alternative
to Cheddar, use
a mixture of your
favorite cheeses
as part of the bake
topping.

Potato, Beef & Peanut Pot

INGREDIENTS

1 tbsp vegetable oil
¼ cup butter
1 lb/450 g lean beef
   steak, cut into
   thin strips
1 onion, halved and
   sliced
2 garlic cloves, crushed
2 large waxy potatoes,
   cubed
½ tsp paprika
4 tbsp crunchy peanut
   butter
2½ cups beef bouillon
1 oz/25 g unsalted
   peanuts
2 tsp light soy sauce
1¾ oz/50 g snap peas
1 red bell pepper, cut
   into strips
parsley sprigs, to
   garnish (optional)

❶ Heat the oil and butter in a flameproof casserole dish.

❷ Add the beef strips to the dish and panfry them gently for 3–4 minutes, stirring and turning the meat until it is sealed on all sides.

❸ Add the onion and garlic, and cook for an additional 2 minutes, stirring constantly.

❹ Add the potato cubes, and cook for 3–4 minutes, or until they begin to brown slightly.

❺ Stir in the paprika and peanut butter, then blend in the beef bouillon a little at a time. Bring the mixture to a boil, stirring frequently.

❻ Finally, add the peanuts, soy sauce, snap peas, and red bell pepper.

❼ Cover the pan, and cook over a low heat for 45 minutes, or until the beef is cooked through.

❽ Serve the dish hot, perhaps garnished with parsley sprigs.

 very easy

 serves 4

 5 minutes

 1 hour

Veal Italienne

INGREDIENTS

¼ cup butter
1 tbsp olive oil
1½ lb/675 g potatoes,
    cubed
4 veal escalopes,
    weighing about
    6 oz/175 g each
1 onion, cut into 8
    wedges
2 garlic cloves, crushed
2 tbsp all-purpose flour
2 tbsp tomato paste
⅔ cup red wine
1¼ cups chicken
    bouillon
8 ripe tomatoes, peeled,
    seeded, and diced
1 oz/25 g pitted black
    olives, halved
2 tbsp chopped fresh
    basil
salt and pepper
fresh basil leaves,
    to garnish

❶ Heat the butter and oil in a large skillet. Add the potato cubes, and cook for 5–7 minutes, stirring frequently, until they begin to brown.

❷ Remove the potatoes from the skillet with a perforated spoon, and set aside.

❸ Place the veal in the skillet and panfry for 2–3 minutes on each side until sealed. Remove the veal from the skillet and set aside.

❹ Add the onion and garlic to the skillet, and panfry for 2–3 minutes.

❺ Add the flour and tomato paste, and cook for 1 minute, stirring. Blend in the red wine and chicken bouillon a little at a time, stirring to make a smooth sauce.

❻ Return the potatoes and veal to the skillet. Stir in the tomatoes, olives, and chopped basil, and season with salt and pepper.

❼ Transfer to a casserole dish and cook in a preheated oven, 350°F/180°C for 1 hour, or until the potatoes and veal are cooked through. Serve the dish hot, garnished with basil leaves.

 very easy

 serves 4

 25 minutes

 1 hour
20 minutes

Lamb Hot Pot

INGREDIENTS

675 g/1½ lb best end
of neck lamb cutlets
2 lamb's kidneys
1½ lb/675 g waxy
potatoes, scrubbed
and sliced thinly
1 large onion,
sliced thinly
2 tbsp chopped
fresh thyme
⅔ cup lamb bouillon
2 tbsp butter, melted
salt and pepper
fresh thyme sprigs,
to garnish

very easy

serves 4

15 minutes

2 hours

❶ Remove any excess fat from the lamb. Skin and core the kidneys, and cut them into slices.

❷ Arrange a layer of potatoes in the base of a 3 pint/ 1.8 liter ovenproof dish.

❸ Arrange the lamb neck cutlets on top of the potatoes, and cover with the sliced kidneys, onion, and chopped fresh thyme.

❹ Pour the lamb bouillon over the meat, and season to taste with salt and pepper.

❺ Layer the remaining potato slices on top, overlapping to cover the meat and sliced onion completely.

❻ Brush the potato slices with the butter, cover the dish, and cook in a preheated oven, 350°F/180°C, for 1½ hours.

❼ Remove the lid and cook for another 30 minutes until golden brown on top.

❽ Garnish with fresh thyme sprigs and serve hot.

COOK'S TIP

Oysters are traditionally, also included in this tasty hotpot. Add them to the layers along with the kidneys, if wished.

Potato & Pepperoni Pizza

very easy

serves 4

20 minutes

45 minutes

❶ Grease and flour a 9 inch/23 cm pizza pan.

❷ Cook the diced potatoes in a pan of boiling water for 10 minutes, or until cooked through. Drain, and mash until smooth. Transfer the mashed potato to a mixing bowl, and stir in the butter, garlic, herbs, and egg.

❸ Spread the mixture into the prepared pizza pan. Cook in a preheated oven, 425°F/225°C, for 7–10 minutes, or until the pizza base begins to set.

❹ Mix the passata and tomato paste together and spoon the mixture over the pizza base, to within ½ inch/1 cm of the edge of the base.

❺ Arrange the pepperoni, bell peppers, mushrooms, and olives on top of the passata.

❻ Scatter the mozzarella cheese on top of the pizza. Cook in the oven for 20 minutes or until the base is cooked through and the cheese has melted on top. Serve the pizza hot with a mixed salad.

Potato, Tomato & Sausage Panfry

INGREDIENTS

2 large potatoes, sliced
1 tbsp vegetable oil
8 flavored sausages
1 red onion, cut into 8
1 tbsp tomato paste
⅔ cup passata
⅔ cup red wine
2 large tomatoes,
    each cut into 8
6 oz/175 g broccoli
    florets, blanched
2 tbsp chopped
    fresh basil
salt and pepper
shredded fresh basil,
    to garnish

very easy

serves 4

5 minutes

30 minutes

COOK'S TIP
Broccoli adds a
splash of color to
this dish, but other
vegetables may be
used. Canned plum
tomatoes may be
substituted for
passata.

❶ Cook the sliced potatoes in a pan of boiling water for 7 minutes. Drain thoroughly and set aside.

❷ Meanwhile, heat the oil in a large skillet. Add the sausages and panfry for 5 minutes, turning the sausages frequently to ensure that they are browned on all sides.

❸ Add the onion pieces to the skillet and continue to cook for another 5 minutes, stirring the mixture frequently.

❹ Stir in the tomato paste, the red wine, and the passata, and mix together well. Add the tomatoes, broccoli florets, and chopped basil to the panfry, and mix carefully.

❺ Add the parboiled potato slices to the skillet. Cook the mixture for about 10 minutes, or until the sausages are cooked through. Season to taste with salt and pepper.

❻ Garnish the panfry with shredded basil leaves, and serve hot, directly from the skillet, or transfer to a serving plate before sprinkling with the garnish.

Creamy Chicken & Potato Casserole

INGREDIENTS

2 tbsp vegetable oil
¼ cup butter
4 chicken portions,
    about 8 oz/225 g
    each
2 leeks, sliced
1 garlic clove, crushed
4 tbsp all-purpose flour
3¾ cups chicken
    bouillon
1¼ cups dry white wine
4½ oz/125 g baby
    carrots, halved
    lengthwise
4½ oz/125 g baby corn,
    halved lengthwise
1 lb/450 g small new
    potatoes
1 bouquet garni
⅔ cup heavy cream
salt and pepper

❶ Heat the oil in a large skillet. Cook the chicken for 10 minutes, turning until browned evenly. Transfer the chicken to a casserole dish using a perforated spoon.

❷ Add the leek and garlic to the skillet, and panfry for 2–3 minutes, stirring. Stir in the flour and cook for another minute. Remove the skillet from the heat, and stir in the bouillon and wine. Season well.

❸ Return the skillet to the heat, and bring the mixture to a boil. Stir in the carrots, corn, potatoes, and bouquet garni.

❹ Transfer the mixture to the casserole dish. Cover the casserole dish, and cook in a preheated oven, 350°F/180°C, for about 1 hour.

❺ Remove the casserole dish from the oven and stir in the cream. Return the casserole dish to the oven, uncovered, and cook for another 15 minutes. Remove the bouquet garni and discard. Taste, and adjust the seasoning if necessary. Serve the casserole with plain rice or fresh vegetables, such as broccoli.

 very easy

 serves 4

 5 minutes

 1 hour
10 minutes

Potato, Beef & Leek Pasties

INGREDIENTS

8 oz/225 g waxy
   potatoes, diced
1 small carrot, diced
8 oz/225 g beef steak,
   cubed
1 leek, sliced
8 oz/225 g readymade
   pie dough
1 tbsp butter
salt and pepper
1 egg, beaten

❶ Grease a cookie sheet lightly.

❷ Mix the potatoes, carrots, beef, and leek in a large bowl. Season well with salt and pepper.

❸ Place the pie dough on a lightly floured surface, and divide into 4 equal portions. Roll each portion into an 8 inch/20 cm round.

❹ Spoon the potato mixture along the center of each round, to within ½ inch/1 cm of the edge. Top the mixture with the butter, dividing it equally between the rounds. Brush the pie dough edge with a little of the beaten egg.

❺ Fold the pie dough over to encase the filling, and crimp the edges together.

 easy

 serves 4

10–15 minutes

50 minutes

❻ Transfer the pasties to the prepared cookie sheet, and brush them with the beaten egg.

❼ Cook in a preheated oven, 400°F/200°C, for 20 minutes. Reduce the oven temperature to 325°F/160°C, and bake the pasties for another 30 minutes until cooked.

❽ Serve the pasties with a crisp salad or with onion gravy.

VARIATIONS
Use other types of meat, such as pork or chicken, in the pasties and add chunks of apple in step 2.

Carrot-Topped Beef Pie

INGREDIENTS

1 lb/450 g ground beef
1 onion, chopped
1 garlic clove, crushed
1 tbsp all-purpose flour
1¼ cups beef bouillon
2 tbsp tomato paste
1 celery stick, chopped
3 tbsp chopped fresh
    parsley
1 tbsp Worcestershire
    sauce
1½ lb/675 g mealy
    potatoes, diced
2 large carrots, diced
2 tbsp butter
3 tbsp milk
salt and pepper

 very easy

 serves 4

 10 minutes

1 hour 5 minutes

❶ Cook the beef in a large skillet over a high heat for 3–4 minutes or until sealed. Add the onion and garlic, and cook for another 5 minutes, stirring.

❷ Add the flour and cook for 1 minute. Gradually blend in the beef bouillon and the tomato paste. Stir in the celery, 1 tablespoon of the parsley, and the Worcestershire sauce. Season to taste with salt and pepper.

❸ Bring the mixture a boil, then reduce the heat, and simmer for 20–25 minutes. Spoon the beef mixture into a 5 cup pie dish.

❹ Meanwhile, cook the potatoes and carrots in a pan of boiling water for 10 minutes. Drain well, and mash them. Stir the butter, milk, and the remaining parsley into the potato and carrot mixture, and season.

❺ Spoon the potato on top of the beef mixture to cover it completely. Alternatively, pipe the potato with a piping bag.

❻ Cook the pie in a preheated oven, 375°F/190°C, for 45 minutes or until cooked through. Serve hot.

VARIATIONS
Substitute ground lamb, turkey, or pork for beef, adding appropriate herbs, such as rosemary and sage, to enhance the flavor.

Potato, Sausage & Onion Pie

INGREDIENTS

*2 large waxy potatoes,
    unpeeled, and sliced*
2 tbsp butter
*4 thick pork and herb
    sausages*
1 leek, sliced
2 garlic cloves, crushed
*⅔ cup vegetable
    bouillon*
*⅔ cup hard cider,
    or unsweetened
    apple juice*
*2 tbsp chopped
    fresh sage*
2 tbsp cornstarch
4 tbsp water
*¾ cup sharp cheese,
    grated*
salt and pepper

 very easy

 serves 4

 5–10 minutes

 40 minutes

VARIATIONS
Other vegetables,
such as broccoli or
cauliflower, can be
added to the filling.
White wine may be
substituted for hard
cider or apple juice.

❶ Cook the sliced potatoes in a pan of boiling water for 10 minutes. Drain and set aside.

❷ Meanwhile, melt the butter in a skillet and panfry the sausages for 8–10 minutes, turning them frequently so that they brown on all sides. Remove the sausages from the skillet and cut them into thick slices.

❸ Add the leek, garlic, and sausage slices to the skillet, and cook for 2–3 minutes.

❹ Add the vegetable bouillon, hard cider or unsweetened apple juice to the skillet with the chopped sage. Season with salt and pepper. Blend the cornstarch with the water. Stir it into the skillet and bring to a boil, stirring until the sauce is thick and clear. Spoon the mixture into a pie dish.

❺ Layer the potato slices on top of the sausage mixture to cover it completely. Season with salt and pepper and sprinkle the grated cheese over the top.

❻ Cook the pie in a preheated oven, 375°F/190°C, for 25–30 minutes or until the potatoes are cooked and the cheese is golden brown. Serve the pie hot.

Smoked Fish Pie

INGREDIENTS

2 tbsp olive oil
1 onion, chopped finely
1 leek, sliced thinly
1 carrot, diced
1 celery stick, diced
½ cup button
    mushrooms, halved
grated zest 1 lemon
12 oz/350 g smoked
    cod, skinned, boned,
    and cut into cubes
12 oz/350 g white fish,
    skinned, boned, and
    cut into cubes
8 oz/225 g cooked,
    peeled shrimp
2 tbsp chopped parsley
1 tbsp chopped fresh dill
salt and pepper

SAUCE
2 tbsp butter
⅓ cup all-purpose flour
1 tsp mustard powder
2½ cups milk
½ cup Gruyère cheese,
    grated

TOPPING
1 lb 8 oz/675 g
    potatoes, unpeeled
¼ cup butter, melted
¼ cup Gruyère cheese,
    grated

very easy

serves 4

35–40 minutes

1 hour
20 minutes

❶ To make the sauce, melt the butter in a pan and add the flour and mustard. Stir until smooth and cook over a low heat for 2 minutes without coloring. Beat in the milk until smooth. Simmer gently for 2 minutes, then stir in the cheese until smooth. Remove from the heat. Stretch plastic wrap over the surface of the sauce to prevent a skin forming. Set aside.

❷ Meanwhile, boil the potatoes, unpeeled, in salted water for 15 minutes. Drain and set aside to cool.

❸ Heat the oil in a clean skillet. Add the onion and cook for 5 minutes until softened. Add the leek, carrot, celery, and mushrooms. Cook for 10 minutes, until the vegetables have softened. Stir in the lemon zest and cook briefly.

❹ Add the vegetables, fish, shrimp, parsley, and dill to the skillet, and season. Transfer to a greased casserole dish.

❺ Peel the cooled potatoes, grate coarsely, and mix with the melted butter. Cover the filling with the grated potato, and sprinkle with the grated Gruyère cheese.

❻ Cover loosely with foil, and bake in a preheated oven at 400°F/200°C for 30 minutes. Remove the foil, and bake for 30 minutes more. Serve while the filling is still bubbling.

Herring & Potato Pie

INGREDIENTS

1 tbsp Dijon mustard
½ cup butter, softened
1 lb/450 g herrings,
*   filleted*
1 lb 10 oz/750 g
*   potatoes*
2 cooking apples,
*   sliced thinly*
1 large onion, sliced
1 tsp chopped fresh
*   sage*
2½ cups hot fish
*   bouillon*
1 cup crustless ciabatta
*   bread crumbs*
salt and pepper
parsley sprigs, to
*   garnish*

extremely easy

serves 4

15–20 minutes

1 hour 5 minutes

VARIATION
If herrings are unavailable, substitute mackerel, or sardines.

❶ Mix the mustard with 2 tablespoons of the butter until smooth. Spread this mixture over the cut sides of the herring fillets. Season and roll up the fillets. Set aside. Grease a 9 inch/23 cm pie pan generously with some of the remaining butter.

❷ Slice the potatoes thinly, using a mandolin if possible. Blanch for 3 minutes in plenty of boiling, salted water until just tender. Drain well, refresh under cold water, and pat dry.

❸ Melt 2 tablespoons of the remaining butter in a skillet and add the onion. Cook gently for 8–10 minutes until soft but not colored. Remove from the heat and set aside.

❹ Put half the potato slices into the bottom of the pie dish with some seasoning, then add half the apple and half the onion. Put the herring fillets on top of the onion and sprinkle with the sage. Repeat the layers in reverse order, ending with potato. Season well and add enough hot bouillon to reach halfway up the sides of the dish.

❺ Melt the remaining butter and stir in two-thirds of the bread crumbs until well combined. Sprinkle the rest of the bread crumbs over the pie. Bake in the oven, at 375°F/190°C for 40–50 minutes, until the top is golden and the herrings are cooked through. Serve garnished with parsley.

Luxury Fish Pie

½ cup butter
3 shallots, chopped
2 cups button mush-
    rooms, halved
2 tbsp dry white wine
2 lb/900 g live mussels,
    scrubbed and bearded
1 pint/600 ml vegetable
    bouillon
10½ oz/300 g monkfish
    fillet, cubed
10½ oz/300 g skinless
    cod fillet, cubed
10½ oz/300 g skinless
    lemon sole
    fillet, cubed
4 oz/115 g jumbo
    shrimp, peeled
¼ cup all-purpose flour
¼ cup heavy cream

POTATO TOPPING
3 lb 5oz/1.5 kg floury
    potatoes, cubed
¼ cup butter
2 egg yolks
½ cup milk
pinch freshly grated
    nutmeg
salt and pepper
fresh parsley, to garnish

❶ Melt one third of the butter in a skillet, add the shallots, and panfry until soft. Add the mushrooms and cook for 2 minutes. Add the wine and simmer until it has evaporated. Transfer to a large, shallow ovenproof dish, and set aside.

❷ Put the mussels in a large pan, cover, and cook for 3–4 minutes. Discard any that remain closed. Drain, reserving the cooking liquid. When cool enough, remove the mussels from their shells, and add to the mushrooms.

❸ Bring the bouillon to a boil, add the monkfish, and poach for 2 minutes. Add the cod, sole, and shrimp. Poach for 2 minutes, then add to the mussels and mushrooms.

❹ Melt the remaining butter in a pan, add the flour, stir until smooth, and cook for 2 minutes. Stir in the bouillon and mussel liquid gradually. Add the cream and simmer for 15 minutes, stirring. Season to taste and pour over the fish.

❺ To make the topping, boil the potatoes for 15–20 minutes until tender. Drain well and mash with the butter, egg, milk, nutmeg, and seasoning. Pipe over the fish.

❻ Bake the finished fish pie in a preheated oven at 400°F/ 200°C for 30 minutes. Serve hot, garnished with parsley.

 very easy

 serves 4

 10 minutes

 1 hour
10 minutes

Potato-Topped Cod

INGREDIENTS

¼ cup butter
4 waxy potatoes, sliced
1 large onion,
    chopped finely
1 tsp wholegrain
    mustard
1 tsp garam masala
pinch of chili powder
1 tbsp chopped fresh dill
1¼ cups fresh bread
    crumbs
4 cod fillets, about
    6 oz/175 g each
½ cup Gruyère cheese,
    grated
salt and pepper
fresh dill sprigs,
    to garnish

 very easy

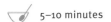 serves 4

 5–10 minutes

🕐 35 minutes

❶ Melt half of the butter in a skillet. Add the potatoes and panfry for 5 minutes, turning until they are browned all over. Remove the potatoes from the skillet with a perforated spoon, transfer to a plate, and set aside.

❷ Add the remaining butter to the skillet and stir in the onion, mustard, garam masala, chili powder, chopped dill, and bread crumbs. Panfry for 1–2 minutes, stirring constantly to mix the ingredients well.

❸ Layer half of the potatoes in the base of an ovenproof dish, and place the cod fillets on top. Cover the cod fillets with the rest of the potato slices. Season to taste with salt and pepper.

❹ Spoon the spicy mixture from the skillet over the potatoes and sprinkle with the grated cheese.

❺ Cook in a preheated oven, 400°F/200°C, for 20–25 minutes or until the topping is golden and crisp and the fish is cooked through. Garnish the dish with fresh dill sprigs, and serve at once.

COOK'S TIP
This dish is ideal served with baked vegetables, which can be cooked in the oven at the same time.

Layered Fish & Potato Pie

extremely easy

serves 4

10 minutes

55 minutes

❶ Cook the sliced potatoes in a pan of boiling water for 10 minutes. Drain and set aside.

❷ Meanwhile, melt the butter in a pan, add the onion, and cook gently for 3–4 minutes.

❸ Add the flour and cook for 1 minute. Blend in the milk and cream, and bring to a boil, stirring until the sauce has thickened.

❹ Arrange half of the potato slices in the base of a shallow ovenproof dish.

❺ Add the fish, diced bell pepper, and broccoli to the sauce, and cook over a low heat for 10 minutes. Season with salt and pepper, then spoon the mixture over the layer of potato slices in the dish.

❻ Arrange the remaining potato slices in a layer over the fish mixture. Sprinkle the Parmesan cheese over the top.

❼ Cook in a preheated oven, 350°F/180°C, for about 30 minutes or until the potatoes are cooked and the top of the pie is golden.

COOK'S TIP
Choose your favorite combination of fish, adding salmon or various shellfish for special occasions.

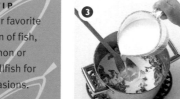
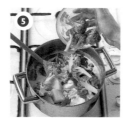

Potato, Tuna & Cheese Quiche

INGREDIENTS

1 lb/450 g mealy
   potatoes, diced
2 tbsp butter
6 tbsp all-purpose flour

FILLING
1 tbsp vegetable oil
1 shallot, chopped
1 garlic clove, crushed
1 red bell pepper, diced
6 oz/175 g canned tuna
   in brine, drained
1¾ oz/50 g canned
   corn, drained
⅔ cup milk
3 eggs, beaten
1 tbsp chopped fresh dill
½ cup sharp cheese,
   grated
salt and pepper

TO GARNISH
fresh dill sprigs
lemon wedges

❶ Boil the potatoes in a pan of salted water for 10 minutes, or until tender. Drain and mash the potatoes. Add the butter and flour, and mix to form a dough.

❷ Knead the potato dough on a floured surface to mix it thoroughly, and press the mixture into an 8 in/20 cm flan shell. Prick the base with a fork. Line with baking parchment and baking beans, and bake blind in a preheated oven, 400°F/200°C, for 20 minutes.

❸ Heat the oil in a skillet, add the onion, garlic, and bell pepper, and cook gently for 5 minutes. Drain well and spoon into the flan shell. Flake the tuna and arrange it over the top, with the corn.

❹ Pour the milk into a bowl, add the eggs and chopped dill, and mix well. Season with salt and pepper.

❺ Pour the egg and dill mixture into the flan shell, then sprinkle the grated cheese on top.

❻ Bake in the oven for 20 minutes or until the filling has set. Garnish the quiche with fresh dill and lemon wedges. Serve with mixed vegetables or salad.

 easy

 serves 4

 20 minutes

 1 hour

Vegetable Hot Pot

INGREDIENTS

2 large potatoes,
   sliced thinly
2 tbsp vegetable oil
1 red onion, halved
   and sliced
1 leek, sliced
2 garlic cloves, crushed
1 carrot, cut into chunks
3½ oz/100 g broccoli
   florets
3½ oz/100 g cauliflower
   florets
2 small turnips,
   cut into fourths
1 tbsp all-purpose flour
3½ cups vegetable
   bouillon
⅔ cup hard cider
1 eating apple, sliced
2 tbsp chopped sage
pinch of cayenne pepper
½ cup Cheddar cheese,
   grated
salt and pepper

❶ Cook the potato slices in a pan of boiling water for 10 minutes. Drain thoroughly, and reserve.

❷ Heat the oil in a large saucepan, add the onion, leek, and garlic, and sauté for 2–3 minutes, stirring now and again. Add the remaining vegetables and sauté for another 3–4 minutes, stirring.

❸ Stir in the flour and cook for 1 minute. Add the bouillon and hard cider little by little, stirring, then bring the mixture to a boil. Add the apple, sage, and cayenne pepper, and season. Remove the pan from the heat. Transfer the vegetables to an ovenproof dish.

❹ Arrange the potato slices on top of the vegetables, then sprinkle the cheese on top of the potato slices.

❺ Cook the hot pot in a preheated oven, 375°F/190°C, for 30–35 minutes, or until the potato is golden brown and becoming crisp at the edges. Serve immediately.

 extremely easy

 serves 4

 25 minutes

 1 hour

Cauliflower Bake

INGREDIENTS

1 lb/450 g cauliflower,
    broken into florets
2 large potatoes, cubed
3½ oz/100 g cherry
    tomatoes

SAUCE
2 tbsp butter or
    margarine
1 leek, sliced
1 garlic clove, crushed
3 tbsp all-purpose flour
1¼ cups milk
¾ cup mixed grated
    cheese, such as
    Cheddar, Parmesan,
    or Gruyère
½ tsp paprika
2 tbsp chopped flat-leaf
    parsley
salt and pepper
chopped fresh parsley,
    to garnish

❶ Cook the cauliflower in a pan of boiling water for 10 minutes. Drain well and reserve. Meanwhile, cook the potatoes in a pan of boiling water for 10 minutes, then drain, and reserve.

❷ To make the sauce, melt the butter or margarine in a pan, and sauté the leek and garlic for 1 minute. Add the flour and cook, stirring constantly, for 1 minute. Remove the pan from the heat and stir in the milk a little at a time, with ½ cup of the cheese, the paprika, and the parsley. Return the pan to the heat and bring to a boil, stirring. Season with salt and pepper to taste.

❸ Spoon the cauliflower into a deep, ovenproof dish. Add the cherry tomatoes and top with the potatoes. Pour the sauce over the potatoes and sprinkle the remaining cheese over the top.

❹ Bake in a preheated oven, 350°F/180°C, for 20 minutes or until the vegetables are cooked through and the cheese is golden brown and bubbling. Garnish with chopped, fresh parsley and serve immediately.

extremely easy

serves 4

10 minutes

40 minutes

Potato-Topped Vegetables in Wine

INGREDIENTS

1 carrot, diced
6 oz/175 g cauliflower
　florets
6 oz/175 g broccoli
　florets
1 fennel bulb, sliced
2¾ oz/75 g green
　beans, halved
2 tbsp butter
¼ cup all-purpose flour
⅔ cup vegetable
　bouillon
⅔ cup dry white wine
⅔ cup milk
2 tbsp chopped
　fresh sage
6 oz/175 g chestnut
　mushrooms, cut into
　fourths

TOPPING

4 mealy potatoes, diced
2 tbsp butter
4 tbsp plain yogurt
4 tbsp grated Parmesan
　cheese
1 tsp fennel seeds
salt and pepper

❶ Cook the carrot, cauliflower, broccoli, fennel, and green beans in a pan of boiling water for 10 minutes, or until just tender. Drain the vegetables thoroughly and set aside.

❷ Melt the butter in a pan and stir in the flour. Cook for 1 minute, then remove from the heat. Stir in the bouillon, wine, and milk, and bring to a boil, stirring until thickened. Stir in the reserved vegetables, mushrooms, and sage.

❸ Meanwhile, make the topping. Cook the diced potatoes in a separate pan of boiling water for 10–15 minutes or until cooked through. Drain the potatoes and mash with the butter, yogurt, and half of the cheese. Stir the fennel seeds into the mixture.

❹ Transfer the vegetable mixture into a 4 cup pie dish, then spoon the potato over the top, or pipe it on, using a piping bag, to cover the filling completely. Sprinkle the remaining cheese on top. Cook in a preheated oven, 375°F/190°C, for 30–35 minutes or until the topping is golden. Serve the dish piping hot.

 very easy

 serves 4

 20 minutes

 1 hour,
15 minutes

Nutty Harvest Loaf

INGREDIENTS

1 lb/450 g mealy
   potatoes, diced
2 tbsp butter
1 onion, chopped
2 garlic cloves, crushed
4½ oz/125 g unsalted
   peanuts
2¾ oz/75 g fresh white
   bread crumbs
1 egg, beaten
2 tbsp chopped fresh
   cilantro
⅔ cup vegetable
   bouillon
2¾ oz/75 g closed cap
   mushrooms, sliced
1¾ oz/50 g sun-dried
   tomatoes, sliced
salt and pepper

SAUCE
⅔ cup lowfat cream
   or ricotta cheese
2 tsp tomato paste
2 tsp clear honey
2 tbsp chopped fresh
   cilantro

❶ Grease a 1 lb/450 g loaf pan. Cook the potatoes in a pan of boiling water for 10 minutes until cooked through. Drain well, mash, and set aside.

❷ Melt half of the butter in a skillet. Add the onion and garlic, and fry gently for 2–3 minutes until soft. Set aside. Chop the nuts finely, or blend them in a food processor for 30 seconds with the bread crumbs.

❸ Mix the chopped nuts and the bread crumbs into the potatoes with the egg, cilantro, and vegetable bouillon. Stir in the onion and garlic, and mix well.

❹ Melt the remaining butter in the skillet, add the sliced mushrooms, and panfry for 2–3 minutes.

❺ Press half of the potato mixture into the base of the loaf pan. Spoon the mushrooms on top, and sprinkle with the sun-dried tomatoes. Spoon the remaining potato mixture on top and smooth the surface. Cover the pan with aluminum foil, and bake in a preheated oven, 350°F/190°C, for 1 hour or until firm to the touch.

❻ Meanwhile, mix the sauce ingredients together. Cut the loaf into slices, and serve them warm with the sauce.

 very easy

 serves 4

 20 minutes

 1 hour
20 minutes

❸

❺

❺

Light Meals, Side Dishes & Salads

Light dishes also need to be filling and satisfying, and potato dishes are ideal. Tuna Fish Cakes, served with a simple, homemade tomato sauce, are popular with adults and children, and need only a salad garnish to make an attractive meal. A tomato sauce is also served with Sweet Potato Cakes, but in this dish it has the spicy flavors of Thai cooking—garlic, ginger, lime juice, and cilantro. The recipes in this section include Spain's versatile snack, the *tortilla de patatas* or potato omelet, ideal for a picnic, and crisp little Shrimp Röstis with Cherry Tomato Salsa.

Spanish Tortilla

INGREDIENTS

½ cup/25 g olive oil
1 lb 4 oz/550 g
    potatoes, sliced
1 large onion, sliced
1 large garlic clove,
    crushed
6 large eggs
salt and pepper

❶ Heat a 10 inch/25 cm skillet, preferably non-stick, over a high heat, pour in the oil, and heat. Lower the heat and add the potatoes, onion, and garlic. Cook for 15–20 minutes, stirring frequently, until the potatoes are tender.

❷ Beat the eggs in a large bowl, and season with salt and pepper. Using a slotted spoon, transfer the potatoes and onion to the bowl of eggs. Pour the excess oil in the skillet into a heatproof pitcher, then scrape the base of the skillet.

❸ Add 2 tablespoons of the oil in the pitcher to the skillet, and reheat. Pour in the potato mixture, smoothing the vegetables into an even layer. Cook for 5 minutes, or until the base is set, shaking the skillet occasionally.

❹ Loosen the sides of the tortilla with a spatula. Place a large plate over the skillet, and invert the tortilla onto it.

❺ Add 1 tablespoon of the reserved oil to the skillet, and reheat it. Slide the tortilla back into the skillet, cooked-side up. Use the spatula to press the sides down. Continue cooking over a medium heat for 3–5 minutes until set.

❻ Slide the tortilla onto a serving plate. Let it cool for 5 minutes before cutting and serving.

extremely easy

serves 4

10 minutes
40 minutes,
plus 5 minutes
to stand

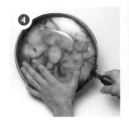

Spicy Potato & Rice Pilaf

INGREDIENTS

1 cup basmati rice,
  soaked in cold water
  for 20 minutes
2 tbsp vegetable oil
½–¾ tsp cumin seeds
8 oz/225 g potatoes,
  cut into ½ inch/
  2.5 cm pieces
8 oz/225 g frozen peas,
  defrosted
1 green chile, seeded
  and sliced thinly
  (optional)
½ tsp salt
1 tsp garam masala
½ tsp ground turmeric
¼ tsp cayenne pepper
2½ cups water
2 tbsp chopped fresh
  cilantro
1 red onion, finely
  chopped
plain yogurt, to serve

❶ Rinse the soaked rice under cold running water until the water runs clear, then drain and set aside.

❷ Heat the oil in a large heavy-based pan over a medium–high heat. Add the cumin seeds to the pan, and stir for about 10 seconds until the seeds jump and color.

❸ Add the potatoes, peas, and chile, if using, and stir-fry for about 3 minutes until the potatoes begin to soften.

❹ Add the rice and cook, stirring frequently, until it turns translucent. Stir in the salt, garam masala, turmeric, and cayenne pepper, then add the water. Bring to a boil, stirring once or twice, then reduce the heat, cover the pan, and simmer until steam holes cover the surface. Do not stir.

❺ Reduce the heat to very low and, if possible, rest the pan on a ring about 1 inch/2.5 cm above the heat source. Cover the pan and steam for 10 minutes more. Remove from the heat, take off the lid, cover the rice with paper towels, and replace the lid. Let stand for 5 minutes.

❻ Gently fork the rice and potato mixture into a warmed serving bowl and sprinkle with the cilantro and chopped red onion. Serve hot, with yogurt handed round separately.

 very easy

 serves 4

 15 minutes

30 minutes,
plus 5 minutes
to stand

Potatoes in Green Sauce

INGREDIENTS

2 lb 4 oz/1 kg small
    waxy potatoes,
    peeled
1 onion, halved, but
    unpeeled
8 garlic cloves, left
    unpeeled
1 fresh green chile
8 tomatillos, outer
    husks removed, or
    small tart tomatoes
1 cup chicken, meat,
    or vegetable bouillon
½ tsp ground cumin
1 sprig fresh thyme or
    generous pinch
    dried thyme
1 sprig fresh oregano,
    or generous pinch
    dried oregano
2 tbsp vegetable or
    extra-virgin
    olive oil
1 zucchini, coarsely
    chopped
1 bunch fresh cilantro,
    chopped
salt

❶ Put the potatoes in a pan of salted water. Bring to a boil and cook for about 15 minutes, or until almost tender. Do not over-cook them. Drain and set aside.

❷ Meanwhile, char the onion, garlic, chile, and tomatillos or tomatoes lightly in a heavy-based, ungreased skillet. Set aside, and when cool, peel and chop the onion, garlic, and chile, and chop the tomatillos. Put the vegetables in a blender or a food processor with half the bouillon, and process to a purée. Add the cumin, thyme, and oregano.

❸ Heat the oil in a heavy-based skillet. Add the purée and cook over a medium heat for about 5 minutes, stirring, to reduce slightly, and concentrate the flavors.

❹ Add the potatoes and zucchini, and pour in the rest of the bouillon. Add about half the cilantro and cook for 5–10 minutes until the zucchini is tender.

❺ Transfer the vegetables to a serving bowl, and serve sprinkled with the remaining cilantro.

 extremely easy

 serves 4

 15 minutes

 45 minutes

Potatoes with Goat Cheese & Chipotle Cream

INGREDIENTS

2 lb 12 oz/1.25 kg
  baking potatoes,
  peeled and cut into
  chunks
pinch of salt
pinch of sugar
¾ cup lowfat cream or
  ricotta cheese
½ cup vegetable or
  chicken bouillon
3 garlic cloves, chopped
  finely
a few shakes of bottled
  chipotle salsa,
  or ½ dried chipotle,
  reconstituted,
  seeded, and
  sliced thinly
8 oz/225 g goat cheese,
  sliced
1½ cups mozzarella or
  Cheddar cheese,
  grated
⅔ cup Parmesan or
  pecorino cheese,
  grated
salt

❶ Put the potatoes in a pan of water with the salt and sugar. Bring to a boil and cook for about 10 minutes until they are half cooked.

❷ Combine the lowfat cream or ricotta cheese with the bouillon, garlic, and the chipotle salsa.

❸ Arrange half the potatoes in a casserole dish. Pour half the cream sauce over the potatoes and cover with the goat cheese. Top with the remaining potatoes and sauce.

❹ Sprinkle with the grated mozzarella or Cheddar cheese, then with the grated Parmesan or pecorino.

❺ Bake in a preheated oven at 350°F/180°C for 10 minutes or until the potatoes are tender and the cheese topping is lightly golden and crisp in places. Serve immediately.

 extremely easy

 serves 4

 15 minutes

 20 minutes

Tuna Fish Cakes

INGREDIENTS

8 oz/225 g potatoes,
  cubed
1 tbsp olive oil
1 large shallot,
  chopped finely
1 garlic clove,
  chopped finely
1 tsp thyme leaves
7 oz/400 g canned tuna
  in olive oil, drained
grated zest ½ lemon
1 tbsp chopped fresh
  parsley
2–3 tbsp all-purpose
  flour
1 egg, beaten lightly
4 oz/115 g fresh bread
  crumbs
vegetable oil, for
  shallow frying
salt and pepper

QUICK TOMATO SAUCE
2 tbsp olive oil
14 oz/400 g canned
  chopped tomatoes
1 garlic clove, crushed
½ tsp sugar
grated zest ½ lemon
1 tbsp chopped fresh
  basil
salt and pepper

❶ To make the tuna fish cakes, cook the potatoes in boiling salted water for 12–15 minutes, or until tender. Transfer them to a bowl and mash, leaving a few lumps. Set aside.

❷ Heat the oil in a small skillet and cook the shallot gently for 5 minutes until softened. Add the garlic and thyme leaves, and cook for another minute. Let cool slightly, then add to the potatoes with the tuna, lemon zest, parsley, and seasoning. Mix together well but not too smoothly.

❸ Form the mixture into 6–8 cakes. Dip the cakes first in the flour, then in the egg, and then into the bread crumbs to coat them. Refrigerate for 30 minutes.

❹ Meanwhile, make the tomato sauce. Put the olive oil, tomatoes, garlic, sugar, lemon zest, basil, and seasoning into a pan, and bring to a boil. Cover the pan, and simmer gently for 30 minutes.Uncover, and simmer for another 15 minutes until thickened.

❺ Heat enough oil in a skillet to cover the bottom generously. When hot, add the fish cakes in batches and panfry for 3–4 minutes each side until golden and crisp. Drain on paper towels while you fry the remaining fish cakes. Serve hot with the tomato sauce.

very easy

serves 4

5 minutes

1 hour
10 minutes

Shrimp Röstis

INGREDIENTS

12 oz/350 g potatoes
12 oz/350 g celery root
1 carrot
½ small onion
8 oz/225 g cooked,
   peeled shrimp,
   thawed if frozen,
   and drained on
   paper towels
¼ cup all-purpose flour
1 egg, beaten lightly
vegetable oil, for frying
salt and pepper

CHERRY TOMATO
SALSA

8 oz/225 g mixed cherry
   tomatoes, such as
   baby plum, yellow,
   orange, or pear, cut
   into fourths
½ small mango, diced
   finely
1 red chile, seeded and
   chopped finely
½ small red onion,
   chopped finely
1 tbsp chopped cilantro
1 tbsp chopped fresh
   chives
2 tbsp olive oil
2 tsp lemon juice
salt and pepper

 very easy

 serves 4

 10 minutes

 1 hour

❶ To make the salsa, put the tomatoes, mango, chile, red onion, cilantro, chives, olive oil, lemon juice, and seasoning into a bowl, and mix. Set aside for the flavors to infuse.

❷ Using a food processor or the fine blade of a box grater, grate the potatoes, celery root, carrot, and onion finely. Mix the grated vegetables with the shrimp, flour, and egg, then season well with salt and pepper, and set aside.

❸ Divide the shrimp mixture into 8 equal portions. Press each into a greased 4 inch/10 cm cutter (if you only have 1 cutter, simply shape the röstis individually).

❹ Pour a shallow layer of oil into a large skillet, and place over a high heat. When hot, transfer the vegetable cakes, still in the cutters, to the skillet, in batches if necessary. When the oil sizzles underneath, remove the cutter. Fry gently, pressing down with a spatula, for 6–8 minutes on each side, until the röstis are crisp and browned and the vegetables are tender. Drain on paper towels. Serve at once, while still hot, accompanied by the tomato salsa.

Salt Cod Hash

INGREDIENTS

1 lb 10 oz/750 g salt cod
4 eggs
3 tbsp olive oil, plus
  extra for drizzling
8 slices bacon, chopped
1 lb 9 oz/700 g old
  potatoes, diced
8 garlic cloves
8 thick slices good-
  quality white bread
2 plum tomatoes,
  skinned and chopped
2 tsp red wine vinegar
2 tbsp chopped fresh
  parsley, plus extra
  to garnish
salt and pepper
lemon wedges,
  to garnish

❶ Soak the prepared cod in cold water for 2 hours. Drain well. Discard the soaking water. Bring a large pan of water to a boil and add the fish. Remove from the heat and let stand for 10 minutes. Drain the fish on paper towels and flake the flesh. Set aside.

❷ Bring a pan of water to a boil and add the eggs. Simmer the eggs for 7 minutes from when the water returns to a boil for a soft center, 9 minutes for a firm center. Drain the eggs and plunge them in cold water to stop them cooking. When cool, shell the eggs and chop roughly. Set aside.

❸ Heat the oil in a large skillet and add the bacon. Cook over a medium heat for 4–5 minutes until crisp and brown. Remove with a slotted spoon and drain on paper towels. Add the potatoes to the skillet with the garlic and cook over a medium heat for 8–10 minutes until crisp and golden.

❹ Toast the bread on both sides until golden. Drizzle with olive oil, and set aside.

❺ Add the tomatoes, bacon, fish, vinegar, and chopped egg to the potatoes and garlic. Cook for 2 minutes. Stir in the parsley and season to taste. Put the toast on plates, top with hash, and serve with parsley and lemon wedges.

 easy

 serves 4

 10 minutes, plus
2 hours to soak
and 10 minutes
to stand

 30 minutes

Potatoes in Creamed Coconut

INGREDIENTS

1 lb 5 oz/600 g potatoes
1 onion, sliced thinly
2 red bird's eye chiles,
   chopped
½ tsp salt
½ tsp ground black
   pepper
½ cup creamed coconut
1½ cups vegetable or
   chicken bouillon
chopped fresh cilantro
   or basil, to garnish

❶ Peel the potatoes thinly and cut them into cubes about ¾ inch/2 cm on each side.

❷ Place the potatoes in a pan with the onion, chiles, salt, pepper, and creamed coconut. Stir in the bouillon.

❸ Bring to a boil, stirring, then lower the heat, cover, and simmer, stirring occasionally, until the potatoes are tender.

❹ Adjust the seasoning to taste, then sprinkle with chopped cilantro or basil. Serve hot.

 extremely easy

 serves 4

 10 minutes

 15 minutes

COOK'S TIP

If the potatoes are a thin-skinned, or new variety, wash or scrub, and cook them in their skins. This adds extra dietary fiber and nutrients to the dish, and cuts preparation time. Cook baby new potatoes whole.

Potatoes & Spinach Yellow Curry Sauce

INGREDIENTS

2 garlic cloves,
    chopped finely
1 inch/2.5 cm piece
    galangal, chopped
    finely
1 lemon grass stem,
    chopped finely
1 tsp coriander seeds
3 tbsp vegetable oil
2 tsp red curry paste
½ tsp turmeric
scant 1 cup coconut milk
9 oz/250 g potatoes,
    peeled
scant ½ cup vegetable
    bouillon
3 cups young spinach
    leaves
1 small onion, sliced
    thinly into rings

 extremely easy

 serves 4

 5 minutes

 5 minutes

❶ Place the garlic, galangal, lemon grass, and coriander seeds in a mortar and pound with a pestle until a smooth paste forms.

❷ Heat 2 tablespoons of the oil in a wok. Stir in the paste and stir-fry for 30 seconds. Stir in the red curry paste and turmeric, then add the coconut milk and bring to a boil.

❸ Cut the potatoes into ¾ inch/2 cm cubes and add to the wok with the bouillon. Return to a boil, then lower the heat, and simmer, uncovered, for 10–12 minutes until the potatoes are almost tender.

❹ Stir in the spinach and simmer until the leaves wilt.

❺ Meanwhile, cook the onion rings in the remaining oil until they are crisp and golden brown. Arrange them on top of the curry just before serving.

COOK'S TIP

Choose a firm, waxy potato for this dish, one that will keep its shape during cooking, rather than a mealy variety which breaks up during cooking.

Sweet Potato Cake with Soy & Tomato Sauce

INGREDIENTS

2 sweet potatoes,
 about 1 lb 2 oz/500 g
 total weight
2 garlic cloves, crushed
1 small green chile,
 chopped
2 sprigs cilantro,
 chopped
1 tbsp dark soy sauce
all-purpose flour, for
 shaping
vegetable oil, for frying
sesame seeds, for
 sprinkling

SOY & TOMATO SAUCE
2 tsp vegetable oil
1 garlic clove, chopped
 finely
¾ inch/2 cm piece
 ginger, chopped
 finely
3 tomatoes, skinned
 and chopped
2 tbsp dark soy sauce
1 tbsp lime juice
2 tbsp chopped fresh
 cilantro

❶ First make the tomato sauce. Heat the oil in a wok and stir-fry the garlic and ginger for about 1 minute. Add the tomatoes and stir-fry for another 2 minutes. Remove from the heat and stir in the soy sauce, lime juice, and cilantro. Set aside and keep warm.

❷ Peel the sweet potatoes and grate finely (you can do this in a food processor). Place the garlic, chile, and cilantro in a mortar, and crush with a pestle to a smooth paste. Stir in the soy sauce, and mix with the sweet potatoes.

❸ Divide the mixture into 12 equal portions and shape each with your hands into a flat, round patty shape. Dip into flour and pat into shape.

❹ Heat a shallow layer of oil in a wide skillet. Fry the sweet potato cakes over a high heat until they are golden, turning once. Drain on paper towels and sprinkle with sesame seeds. Serve hot, with a spoonful of the tomato sauce.

 extremely easy

 serves 4

 10–15 minutes

 15 minutes

Sweet Potato & Banana Salad

INGREDIENTS

1 lb/450 g sweet
    potatoes, diced
10 tsp butter
1 tbsp lemon juice
1 garlic clove, crushed
1 red bell pepper, diced
1 green bell pepper,
    diced
2 bananas, sliced thickly
2 thick slices white
    bread, crusts
    removed, diced
salt and pepper

DRESSING
2 tbsp clear honey
2 tbsp chopped fresh
    chives
2 tbsp lemon juice
2 tbsp olive oil

 extremely easy

 serves 4

 15 minutes

 20 minutes

❶ Cook the sweet potatoes in a pan of boiling water for 10–15 minutes until tender. Drain thoroughly and reserve. Set aside for later use.

❷ Meanwhile, melt the butter in a skillet. Add the lemon juice, garlic, and bell peppers, and panfry for 3 minutes, turning constantly.

❸ Add the banana slices to the pan and cook for 1 minute. Remove the bananas from the pan with a slotted spoon and stir them into the potatoes.

❹ Add the bread cubes to the skillet and cook them for about 2 minutes, turning frequently until they are golden brown on all sides.

❺ To make the dressing, put all the ingredients in a small pan, mix them well together, and heat until the honey runs.

❻ Spoon the potato mixture into a serving dish and season to taste with salt and pepper. Pour the dressing over the potatoes, and sprinkle the croûtons over the top. Serve the salad immediately, while still warm.

VARIATION
Use firm, slightly underripe bananas in this recipe. They will not turn soft and mushy when fried.

Indian Potato Salad

INGREDIENTS

4 medium mealy
    potatoes, diced
2¾ oz/75 g small
    broccoli florets
1 small mango, diced
4 scallions, sliced
salt and pepper
small cooked spiced
    poppadoms, to serve

DRESSING
½ tsp ground cumin
½ tsp ground coriander
1 tbsp mango chutney
⅔ cup plain yogurt
1 tsp ginger root,
    chopped
2 tbsp chopped fresh
    cilantro

 extremely easy

 serves 4

 25 minutes

 20 minutes

COOK'S TIP
Mix the dressing in
advance and let chill
in the refrigerator
for a few hours to
let a stronger flavor
develop.

❶ Cook the potatoes in a pan of boiling water for about 10 minutes or until tender. Drain and place in a mixing bowl.

❷ Meanwhile, blanch the broccoli florets in a separate pan of boiling water for 2 minutes. Drain well and add to the potatoes in the bowl.

❸ When the potatoes and broccoli have cooled, add the diced mango and sliced scallions. Season to taste with salt and pepper and mix well to combine.

❹ To make the dressing, put all the dressing ingredients in a small bowl and stir well to combine them.

❺ Spoon the dressing over the potato mixture and mix carefully, taking care not to break up the potato dice and the broccoli florets.

❻ Serve the salad at once, perhaps accompanied by small cooked spiced poppadoms.

Potato, Arugula & Apple Salad

INGREDIENTS

2 large potatoes,
   1 lb 5 oz/600 g
   total weight,
   unpeeled and sliced
2 green dessert apples,
   diced
1 tsp lemon juice
1 oz/25 g walnut pieces
4½ oz/125 g goat
   cheese, cubed
5½ oz/150 g arugula
   leaves
salt and pepper

DRESSING
2 tbsp olive oil
1 tbsp red wine vinegar
1 tsp clear honey
1 tsp fennel seeds

extremely easy

serves 4

5 minutes,
plus 15 minutes
to cool

15 minutes

❶ Cook the potatoes, unpeeled, in a pan of boiling water for 15–20 minutes until tender. Drain and let cool. Slice the cooled potatoes, and put the slices in a serving bowl.

❷ Toss the diced apples in the lemon juice, drain, and stir into the cold potatoes.

❸ Add the walnut pieces, cheese cubes, and arugula leaves into the bowl. Toss the salad to mix the ingredients.

❹ To make the dressing, put all the ingredients in a small bowl, and whisk them. Pour the dressing over the salad, and season to taste. Serve the salad immediately.

COOK'S TIP
The apple will discolor if you delay serving the salad. One alternative is to prepare the other ingredients and add the apple just as you are ready to serve.

Potato & Italian Sausage Salad

INGREDIENTS

1 lb/450 g waxy
  potatoes
1 radicchio or lollo rosso
  lettuce
1 green bell pepper,
  sliced
6 oz/175 g Italian
  sausage, sliced
1 red onion, halved
  and sliced
4½ oz/125 g sun-dried
  tomatoes, sliced
2 tbsp shredded fresh
  basil

DRESSING
1 tbsp balsamic vinegar
1 tsp tomato paste
2 tbsp olive oil
salt and pepper

 extremely easy

 serves 4

 25 minutes

25 minutes

❶ Cook the potatoes in a pan of boiling water for 20 minutes or until cooked through. Drain and leave to cool.

❷ Line a large serving plate with the radicchio or lollo rosso lettuce leaves.

❸ Slice the cooled potatoes and arrange them in layers on the lettuce leaves with the sliced green bell pepper, sliced Italian sausage, red onion, sun-dried tomatoes, and shredded fresh basil.

❹ Put the balsamic vinegar, tomato paste, and olive oil into a small bowl, and whisk until combined. Season to taste with salt and pepper. Pour the dressing over the potato salad, and serve immediately.

COOK'S TIP
If you buy jars of sun-dried tomatoes in oil, rinse the oil from the tomatoes and pat them dry on paper towels before using.